Michele Kang

Pioneering Healthcare Innovation-A Visionary Leader in Healthcare Technology

Benny M.Williams

Copyright

All rights reserved. No part of this publication may be reproduced, distributed, or transmitted in any form or by any means, including photocopying, recording, and other electronic or mechanical methods, without prior written permission of the publisher, except in case of briefs quotation embodied in critical reviews and certain other noncommercial uses permitted by copyright law.

Copyright © Benny M. Williams,2024

Table of content

Introduction

Chapter 1: Early Life and Education

Career Beginnings

Chapter 2: Founding Cognosante

Achievements in Healthcare IT

Chapter 3: Philanthropy and Advocacy

Challenges and Triumphs

Chapter 4: Impact and Legacy

Personal Life

Conclusion

Introduction

In the fields of entrepreneurship and healthcare technology, Michele Kang is a pathfinder. Kang has transformed how healthcare systems run, increasing access, efficiency, and results for millions of people as the founding and CEO of Cognosante, a trailblazing company committed to using creative digital solutions to enhance healthcare. By bridging the gap between technology and healthcare to handle some of society's most urgent problems, her vision and leadership have positioned her as one of the most powerful individuals in the business.

Born within a society that valued diligence and knowledge, Kang's early years set the stage for her unwavering motivation and will. From blazing academically to shattering stereotypes in professions dominated by males, her path has been one of tenacity, creativity, and a dedication to change things. Her capacity to mix economic acumen with a thorough awareness of healthcare needs has not only driven her career success but also confirmed her image as a change agent with a heart for service.

The narrative of Michele Kang inspires resiliency and influence. Leader, philanthropist, and advocate of equity in healthcare she keeps empowering people and communities, permanently changing the world. From her modest upbringing to her ascent to become a worldwide known leader, this biography explores the events and principles that define her extraordinary legacy.

Chapter 1: Early Life and Education

Early life and educational events greatly influenced Michele Kang's path to becoming a transforming agent in business leadership and healthcare technology. Her family stressed discipline, education, and the need to help society. Hence, she was raised with principles of diligence and fortitude from early life. Though much of her early life is still secret, Kang grew up in an environment that encouraged her ambition and curiosity. Her background fostered a mindset that, despite obstacles, aimed to break through limits and grab possibilities.

From her early years in school, Kang showed extraordinary critical thinking and learning ability. She was a gifted student who frequently distinguished herself as a committed and top achiever. Her analytical approach to the environment around her and her love of solving problems became clear and guided her interests in disciplines that combined impact, reason, and creativity. Understanding the value of more knowledge as a means of difference-making, Kang studied deliberately to lay the groundwork for a career that would enable her to inspire change and invention.

Her Bachelor of Arts degree in Economics came from the University of Chicago, a place known for encouraging intellectual rigour and autonomous thinking. She polished her knowledge of intricate economic systems and acquired a great analytical ability there. Her schooling in Chicago prepared her to address major systemic issues—a topic that would later define her career in healthcare technology.

Kang's intellectual search did not stop there. Seeking a Master of Public and Private Management (MPPM) at Yale School of Management, driven by a need to increase her knowledge and investigate the junction of business and societal effect, Her attitude to creativity and leadership was much shaped by this program, which stressed leadership, strategic thinking, and multidisciplinary approaches to problem-solving. At Yale, Kang sharpened her capacity to negotiate the complexity of sectors by immersing herself in studies combining corporate ideas with an emphasis on public good.

Career Beginnings

Beginning her career with a mix of ambition, diligence, and a desire to have significant influence in sectors spanning business, technology, and social improvement, Michele Kang's career started in management consulting, a job noted for its rigidity and chances to address challenging problems in many different industries. Early on in her career, this was a vital basis since it gave her the tools, knowledge, and confidence needed to finally redefine leadership and creativity in healthcare technology.

Working with well-known clients, Kang was a consultant helping companies simplify their processes and solve structural inefficiencies. Her experience let her come across many sectors, each with special possibilities and difficulties. She thrived in this high-stress setting in dissecting complex issues and creating workable plans, usually fusing a strong awareness of human elements with data-driven techniques. Her capacity for critical thinking and creative problem-solving set her apart among rising consultants. These early years confirmed her reputation as someone who could produce outcomes while encouraging teamwork and creativity inside groups.

Kang, though, was not happy to just shine in consulting. She aimed to advance from advising roles into positions where she could personally drive and carry out transformation. Her move into corporate leadership signalled the next phase of her life. During this time, one of her key jobs was with Northrop Grumman Corporation, a top worldwide aerospace and defence technology business. Kang joined Northrop Grumman during a turning point in the business and sector overall.

Kang assumed positions at Northrop Grumman that demanded her to oversee challenging teams and spearhead major initiatives. She was essential in creating and implementing cutting-edge technical solutions addressing client-facing as well as internal problems. Her work frequently required negotiating the junction of technology and human systems, where she found means to make procedures more effective, safe, and flexible. Kang gained respect inside the company and opened the path for her climb to more senior leadership roles by rapidly proving herself to be a strategic thinker with an eye for invention.

Her performance at Northrop Grumman was evidence of not only her technical and managerial skills but also of her capacity for visionary and sympathetic leadership. She gave great importance to developing close bonds among her teams and encouraging an outstanding culture of cooperation. This strategy enabled her to spearhead transforming improvements benefiting not only the business but also its stakeholders and customers. Kang distinguishes herself as a leader able to negotiate the complexity of a worldwide company while keeping a people-first approach, therefore inspiring and encouraging others around her.

Though Kang excelled in the business sector, her entrepreneurial energy started to take hold. She recognized chances to solve structural problems in fields underprivileged or failing to keep up with fast technology changes. With its great complexity and significant influence on society, healthcare became her main focus of aspiration. She saw how technology would transform healthcare systems so they would be more fair, accessible, and efficient. This insight would finally cause her to start Cognosante, her own business, a choice that marked the end of her early job experiences and the start of her path as an entrepreneur.

Michele Kang showed throughout her early career a rare mix of technical mastery, strategic vision, and a strong will to bring about significant transformation. Her future success is set up by her capacity to thrive in demanding situations and her readiness to take measured chances. These early years not only sharpened her abilities but also moulded her ideals and goals, arming her to be a transforming leader in the field of healthcare technology. Early in her career, Kang is a story of a tenacious search, flexibility, and a passion for producing answers that matter—a narrative that would only get richer with her later successes.

Chapter 2:Founding Cognosante

Michele Kang's career was defined by the formation of Cognosante in 2008, which also attested to her vision, entrepreneurial energy, and will to have a long-lasting influence on the healthcare sector. After years of shining in management consulting and corporate leadership, Kang realized that the U.S. healthcare system, despite its developments, was confronting great difficulties. Rising healthcare expenditures, inefficiencies in service delivery, and differences in access to care were only a few of the problems that underlined the immediate need for systemic reform. At the time, Kang noticed a chance to solve these problems by including technology and creative ideas in the delivery of healthcare—something not often occurring in the field.

Kang set out to create a business able to solve ongoing problems with her great technological knowledge and love of improving healthcare. Born from her conviction that technology might be the key to providing people throughout the nation with more inexpensive, effective, and easily available healthcare options, Cognosante Kang had the ideal basis to start the business because of her great awareness of the corporate and technology environments as well as her emphasis on people-centred solutions.

Cognosante's original idea was simple: use technology to increase access to and delivery of healthcare. Still, the route to start the business was not without difficulties. Being a woman in a field dominated by men, Kang encountered mistrust and had to overcome many challenges to establish credibility and safe alliances. Notwithstanding these obstacles, her will, and vision for a fairer healthcare system kept her focused. Early on, Cognosante was negotiating the complexity of the healthcare industry, spotting chances where technology may propel change, and developing links with important government agencies and healthcare companies.

Although Kang approached company growth methodically, his approach was driven by a great sense of purpose. She intended to establish a company that could significantly impact people's lives, especially those of underprivileged individuals or those encountering obstacles to healthcare, not only a business. Cognosante started offering solutions meant to modernize the American healthcare system given this aim. The company's offerings varied from supporting healthcare IT infrastructure to assisting in saving administrative expenses to streamlining government health programs and optimizing healthcare management using data analytics. Especially working closely with the Centers for Medicare and Medicaid Services (CMS) and other federal and state organizations, Cognosante provided necessary technical solutions to increase the effectiveness and reach of healthcare initiatives.

Under Kang's direction, Cognosante became well-known very rapidly as a top supplier of healthcare technology solutions. The company was founded on the conviction that technology might enhance the healthcare system in a way that would benefit all users—patients, doctors, and legislators. Organizations throughout the nation could relate to the company's operations, which revolved mostly around unbound customer service, efficiency, and long-term value.

Technical knowledge was only one factor in Kang's success; the other, stressed teamwork, openness, and building an empowering corporate culture. Kang encouraged her staff to think outside the box and welcome obstacles as chances, therefore creating a climate that letsovation and creativity bloom. In terms of projects as well as clients, this strategy produced ongoing expansion. Cognosante quickly broadened its offerings outside government contracts to include alliances with commercial sector companies, therefore increasing its influence throughout the healthcare system.

Under Kang's direction, Cognosante has had a fl Millions of Americans' quality of life directly benefits from the company's efforts with the federal government to modernize Medicare and Medicaid services, enhance the use of healthcare data, and guarantee better coordination of treatment. By emphasizing data analytics and IT solutions, the company has helped companies simplify procedures, enhance decision-making, save healthcare expenses, and improve general patient outcomes.

The success of Cognosante also reflects Kang's relentless dedication to social responsibility. She saw healthcare as having the potential to significantly contribute to society by making sure underprivileged groups got the treatment and attention they were due, not only a commercial possibility. A major component of Cognosante's quick ascent and ongoing success was its all-encompassing approach to business—balancing profitability with purpose.

Growing and spreading its impact in the field of healthcare technology, Cognosante's leadership was progressively acknowledged both inside and outside of the business. She was commended for guiding a business that effectively negotiated the complexity of the healthcare system while fostering creativity and constructive change. Particularly seen through the prism of technology and data-driven solutions, her work has established her as a visionary leader committed to enhancing healthcare for all.

The foundation of Cognosante was more than just the start of a company; it was the expression of Michele Kang's will to significantly influence personal lives and healthcare systems. Cognosante's success has been much aided by her capacity to spot chances for innovation, her tenacity in overcoming challenges, and her unflinching trust in the ability of technology to propel structural change. Cognosante is a shining example today of how a business may integrate social responsibility, technology, and healthcare to produce long-lasting good change. Using Cognosante, Kang has not only transformed healthcare technology but also created the conditions for a time when everyone can access healthcare more fairly, efficiently, and without regard to background.

Achievements in Healthcare IT

The accomplishments in healthcare IT by Michele Kang have been revolutionary. Particularly in the fields of government programs, data analytics, and operational efficiency, she has pioneered various projects that have transformed how healthcare systems operate via her leadership at Cognosante. Her emphasis on combining technology with healthcare has produced simpler procedures, improved healthcare results, and a notable decrease in administrative tasks—ultimately helping to create a more accessible and efficient healthcare system.

Kang's updating of the U.S. government's healthcare programs is among her most important contributions to healthcare IT. Early on in Cognosante's life, the business was crucial in guiding federal agencies—especially the Centers for Medicare and Medicaid Services (CMS)—through the convoluted and sometimes antiquated IT architecture of the government's healthcare initiatives. Serving millions of Americans, these programs were riddled with inefficiencies that often hampered their ability to provide adequate treatment. Kang saw this as a chance to use technology to enhance patient and provider experiences in addition to managing internal operations.

Working with CMS, Cognosante applied advanced data analytics systems and cloud-based solutions to enhance the administration and delivery of healthcare. About important procedures, including claims handling, patient enrollment, and provider contacts with government programs, Kang's organization helped modernize Cognosantaand and helped CMS to greatly increase the speed and dependability of healthcare processes by using cloud technologies, therefore lowering wait times and minimizing mistakes. This effort was essential in increasing the effectiveness of government-sponsored healthcare initiatives so that millions of Americans might more precisely and quickly get the treatment they required.

Under Kang's direction, another significant accomplishment in healthcare IT was the creation of data analytics technologies capable of aggregating and analyzing vast amounts of medical records. This creativity enhanced decision-making at both the personal and institutional levels in addition to helping government organizations and medical professionals better handle patient data. Kang's startup lets healthcare organizations find trends, monitor patient outcomes, and allocate resources more wisely by using predictive analytics. More customized treatment made possible by this data-driven approach helps to expose areas of service delivery lacking, therefore enhancing the quality of treatment available to patients all around.

Kang also significantly helped to advance healthcare interoperability. Modern healthcare depends critically on interoperability, the capacity of many healthcare systems and companies to easily exchange and use data. Using her work with Cognosante, Kang helped create solutions allowing government organizations, insurance companies, and healthcare providers to securely and effectively share important health data. Managing chronic diseases and guaranteeing that patients get ongoing, coordinated treatment across several healthcare environments depend primarily on this interoperability.

Under her direction, Cognosante grew to be a major participant in creating healthcare IT solutions supporting federal regulatory compliance, especially about health information privacy and security. Kang's thorough awareness of the technical and legal environments enabled Cognosante to put mechanisms safeguarding patient data in place that complied with strict legal guidelines including the Health Insurance Portability and Accountability Act (HIPAA). Her emphasis on cybersecurity built confidence in the systems healthcare institutions depended on by helping to protect patient data from data breaches and illegal access.

Apart from her involvement with public healthcare initiatives, Michele Kang was a trailblazer in the commercial sector, working with healthcare companies to maximize their processes using technological applications. From simplifying electronic health records (EHR) to enhancing healthcare claims processing, Cognosante grew to be a reliable partner to many private healthcare providers helping them to adopt IT solutions that enhanced patient care, lowered administrative costs, and improved operational processes. Kang's work was especially important in lessening the load of paper-based procedures so that medical personnel could concentrate more on patient care than on negotiating difficult systems.

Furthermore, Kang's success in healthcare IT was her emphasis on creativity. She was always looking for ways to stretch technological capabilities to enhance the provision of healthcare. Cognosante was leading the way in bringing next-generation technology into healthcare systems from artificial intelligence (AI) to improve diagnosis accuracy to machine learning algorithms to forecast patient demands. These developments not only improved the efficiency of healthcare but also had a significant influence on patient outcomes, therefore proving the possibility for technology to completely change the sector.

Kang is well-known both inside and outside of the healthcare IT sector for her success in this field. Many have praised her leadership and vision in using technology to change the way healthcare is delivered. Her leadership at Cognosante has had a long-lasting effect on lowering expenses, improving general patient experience, and increasing healthcare access.

By making sure healthcare is more efficient, fair, and effective, Michele Kang's successes in healthcare IT have not only advanced the discipline but also enhanced the lives of innumerable people. < Her contributions show how creative ideas can be used to address difficult social issues and testify to the ability of technology to promote institutional transformation. Her dedication to transforming healthcare using technology keeps Cognosante's success going as she leads the firm and helps to change the direction of healthcare in the United States and worldwide.

Chapter 3:Philanthropy and Advocacy

As powerful as her commercial success is, Michele Kang's charitable efforts and activism show her strong commitment to returning to society and producing enduring, constructive change. Particularly in healthcare access, education, and diversity, she has championed causes near to her heart using her success in healthcare IT as a platform. Using her charitable endeavours, Kang has shown a dedication to social responsibility and has laboured assiduously to solve important problems compromising underprivileged areas.

Expanding access to healthcare for underprivileged and underprivileged groups is one of Kang's most important charity endeavours. Leading in healthcare technology, she has long seen the differences in healthcare delivery among minorities and other vulnerable groups as well as in rural and low-income regions. Kang's enthusiasm for bettering healthcare access has driven her to back many projects meant to correct these discrepancies. Her advocacy of more equitable healthcare policies and her work with Cognosante have been crucial in making sure underprivileged groups get the treatment they need. Beyond her work, Kang has participated in several nonprofit projects and activities offering resources, education, and healthcare services to people most likely facing the toughest obstacles in obtaining adequate healthcare. Her charitable endeavours in this field have concentrated on making sure everyone from all walks of life may get the treatment they are due. Socio-economic background aside.

Apart from her attention to healthcare access, Kang has been a strong supporter of diversity and inclusion in the fields of technology and healthcare. Kang, a woman of colour working in a field dominated by men, personally knows the difficulties underprivileged groups encounter. In the healthcare and technology sectors, she has advocated policies and practices that support diversity, equity, and inclusion using her voice and position. Her advocacy efforts have included helping projects aiming at racial inclusiveness, gender equality, and women's empowerment in leadership roles. Kang has been a strong advocate of increasing chances for women—especially women of colour—in the technology and business sectors, where they have historically been underrepresented. She has pushed for mentoring programs, scholarships, and other activities meant to generate equitable chances to remove the obstacles standing in the way of women and minorities developing in these sectors.

Beyond only gender and colour, Kang's advocacy of diversity has included supporting those with impairments. She knows that diversity includes people with different talents in addition to racial and gender variety. In keeping with her dedication to inclusiveness, Kang has helped projects aiming at enhancing employment possibilities and healthcare access for people with disabilities both inside and outside the technology industry. Her work in this field supports her conviction that everyone should have the chance to significantly benefit society regardless of background or physical capability.

Still, another pillar of Kang's charitable activities has been education. She thinks that one of the best ways to stop the cycle of poverty and bring about long-term good change in society is by using quality education. A strong supporter of STEM (science, technology, engineering, and mathematics) education, Kang has participated in multiple projects meant to inspire and empower young people—especially from underprivileged backgrounds—to pursue professions in these disciplines. Where there is a great demand for varied expertise in the tech and healthcare industries, Kang has financed scholarships, mentoring programs, and internships meant to inspire students to explore those fields. Her emphasis on STEM education has helped to close racial and gender gaps in these important fields of research, therefore guaranteeing that the next generation of leaders in technology and healthcare is more varied and inclusive.

Particularly for disadvantaged communities, Kang's advocacy and charitable efforts have also supported initiatives encouraging innovation and entrepreneurship. Knowing that entrepreneurship is a major engine of social change and economic development, she has supported programs allowing aspiring entrepreneurs—especially those from low-income or minority backgrounds—access the tools and knowledge required for success. Using mentoring, startup funding, or facilitating access to corporate networks, Kang has been instrumental in creating an environment where disadvantaged entrepreneurs may flourish.

Furthermore, Kang's charitable activities have involved alliances with various non-profit organizations aiming at public health improvement. She has collaborated with groups tackling important health concerns like mental health, chronic illness control, motherhood, and substance addiction. Through her time, knowledge, and financial support, Kang has made sure that people most in need of these services have them at hand. She has fought to support laws and projects guaranteeing fair access to healthcare for all people, regardless of their socioeconomic level or geographical location as she thinks that health is a basic human right.

The long-lasting impact Kang has had on the projects she supports, as well as her financial gifts, define her significance as a philanthropist. Understanding that group efforts usually provide the best results, she has always seen the value of teamwork. Kang has teamed with other leaders, companies, and communities during her charitable path to create a significant impact.

She is dedicated to collaborating with others to propel systematic transformation since she knows that no one individual or entity can tackle society's most urgent problems by itself.

Apart from her contributions to diversity, education, healthcare, and business, Kang has also been a champion of social justice and environmental sustainability. She has backed projects aiming at lessening environmental damage, especially in areas most impacted by pollution and climate change. Kang's more general advocacy activities reflect her conviction in building a more fair and sustainable society in which people have access to the tools they need to lead a happy, meaningful life.

Using her generosity and advocacy, Michele Kang not only enhances the quality of life for innumerable people but also provides a model for others in the corporate and technological domains. She has shown that people and businesses have obligations to use their influence and resources to make the world a better place and that business success can be paired with a great sense of responsibility to society. Her relentless dedication to healthcare access, education, diversity, and social justice has elevated her not only in the digital sphere but also in the more general struggle for equity and opportunity. Through her charitable activities, Kang keeps leaving a legacy of good change that motivates others to follow in her footsteps and contribute to themselves.

Challenges and Triumphs

Challenges and victories abound on Michele Kang's path to success; each of which has moulded her into the powerful corporate leader and philanthropist she is today. Like many great business owners, Kang encountered major roadblocks in her career, but her tenacity, will, and strategic vision helped her to overcome these difficulties and create a profitable firm while benefiting society.

Breaking into a field dominated by men became one of Kang's main career obstacles. She faced opposition and mistrust as a woman of colour working in the technology and healthcare sectors—fields often controlled by men. Early in her profession, she had to negotiate the belief that women—especially women of colour—lacked the technical knowledge to lead in such sectors. Kang's road was not simple; she had to consistently prove herself in settings that were sometimes dismissive or even biased. She used these obstacles, however, as inspiration to push herself further and demonstrate that leadership, creativity, and knowledge had no gender or ethnic limits rather than being demoralized.

Kang also had to deal with the difficulties of launching a company in a fiercely competitive and often turbulent market concurrently. The healthcare IT sector was changing significantly when she started Cognosante, especially about government reform, digital healthcare, and changing patient expectations. The complexity of the sector and its rules created major obstacles to entrance, therefore making success challenging for newcomers. Still, Kang distinguishes herself from many of her rivals with her thorough awareness of healthcare IT and her skill in negotiating challenging government processes. Her knowledge allowed Cognosante to stand out and draw big clients like the Centers for Medicare and Medicaid Services (CMS) by offering solutions that addressed the specialized difficulties inside healthcare programs, especially those of the federal government.

Scaling a business while preserving its basic ideals and dedication to outstanding service presented another big obstacle for Kang. Managing the company's growth and making sure it could keep satisfying its customers' needs without compromising the calibre of its offerings as Cognosante developed was no small accomplishment. Maintaining a solid company culture, operational challenges, and more pressure all accompany scaling a firm. Even as Cognosante grew to be a significant participant in healthcare IT, Kang had to make sure it stayed creative and agile. This included choosing difficult decisions, assembling the correct team, and building a culture that supported innovation and problem-solving while nevertheless upholding strict standards. Today's success of Cognosante is evidence of Kang's ability to strike a balance between quality and expansion, transforming a little startup into a major industry leader.

Along with these professional difficulties, Kang negotiated personal ones that moulded her leadership approach. Early in her career, she battled the work-life balance many working women experience, especially in high-stakes, high-stress fields. Building a business while raising a family was frequently too much, and Kang had to learn how to balance conflicting goals. She learnt to keep going by striking balance and depending on her solid support system, even if she was not immune to the difficulties of burnout or self-doubt many successful women face in their professions. Her capacity to balance the pressures of her personal and professional life enabled her to develop the resilience and confidence required to run a family and a developing business.

Still, Kang's victories are even more remarkable given these obstacles. Her ability to negotiate the complexity of the healthcare and technology sectors, tenacity, and creative thinking help to explain her success in conquering hardship. Her most important victory was starting Cognosante and seeing it grow to be a top supplier of healthcare IT solutions. Under her direction, the firm gained recognition for its innovative work on government healthcare initiatives, especially in terms of Medicare and Medicaid operation simplification. The delivery of services to millions of Americans was much improved by Cognosante's efforts to modernize healthcare IT systems, and Kang's leadership was essential for the company's survival.

Kang has had a broad influence on the healthcare sector, and her contributions are mostly seen as transforming. Using cloud computing, data analytics, and innovative IT solutions, she worked to update the infrastructure of federal healthcare initiatives and bring them into the digital age. Her leadership helped government initiatives run more effectively, enhancing the fiduciary's quality of life, enhancing expenses and noses, and removing inefficiencies. Her emphasis on healthcare IT solutions helped to greatly increase patient experiences, access to care, and outcomes which she addressed. Cognosante's success in this field is evidence of Kang's capacity to convert her vision into powerful ideas that enhance the quality of living.

Apart from her achievements with Cognosante, Kang has also been quite successful in lobbying and philanthropy. Especially in the tech sector, she has been a vocal supporter of more diversity and inclusion. Many have appreciated her attempts to assist underprivileged people working in the field. Particularly in leadership roles, Kang has been a strong supporter of women of colour and has aggressively sought to provide roadways for others to follow in her footsteps. Using her charitable endeavours, she has given others who might not have had access otherwise funding, mentoring, and chances; so, she has created long-lasting change and effect in the areas she serves.

Her capacity to keep a strong feeling of direction across her career was yet another victory. Kang has always stayed focused on her ultimate aims of enhancing healthcare access and generating possibilities for people despite many obstacles. Her work has been directed by a dedication to social justice and fairness; she has regularly used her position to support the causes she feels are important. Peers and colleagues respect and admire Kang's leadership style, which stresses teamwork, inclusivity, and a constant search for greatness.

When we honour Kang's achievements, we should also consider her part in pioneering other women in business and technology. Her success has opened doors for other women—especially those of colour—to shatter stereotypes and flourish in fields traditionally underrepresented. The inspirational tale of tenacity, resiliency, and the force of leadership Kang's ascent to prominence tells is one.

Michele Kang's narrative is ultimately one of overcoming hardship and realizing great achievement against all the obstacles. Her power and will are shown in her ability to negotiate challenging sectors, run a developing company, and push for equity and inclusion. Her difficulties did not define her; rather, they inspired her will to bring about change and realize her vision for a society more fair and inclusive. Kang's achievements in philanthropy and business have solidified her reputation as one of the most powerful and motivating leaders in healthcare IT and will be felt for years to come.

Chapter 4:Impact and Legacy

The influence and legacy Michele Kang leaves go well beyond her achievements in the field of healthcare IT. Visionary leader and philanthropist Kang has changed not only the field of healthcare technology but also the larger corporate, social, and charitable sectors. Her efforts have made a lasting impression on the industries she has changed, the individuals and communities she has raised, and the healthcare systems she has sought to enhance. Kang's contributions are evidence of her relentless conviction in the ability of creativity, fairness, and access to propel favourable change.

Within the field of healthcare technology, Kang's influence is transforming. She transformed the way healthcare IT solutions are provided, especially to government initiatives like Medicare and Medicaid, as the founding and

CEO of Cognosante. Modernizing these programs, increasing the efficiency of healthcare services, and finally raising the quality of treatment given to millions of Americans depended mostly on her company. For people who depend on government programs for their care, Kang not only enhanced the operational aspect of healthcare but also made it more accessible and efficient by including modern technology including cloud computing, data analytics, and digital solutions.

Working with government agencies to simplify processes and lower inefficiencies, Kang's ability to negotiate the convoluted terrain of healthcare reform was among her most important contributions to the field. She realized that systems interacted to improve the whole health ecosystem and that enhancing healthcare was about building a flawless infrastructure guaranteeing patients received the best possible treatment in addition to offering medical services. Under Kang's direction, Cognosante grew to be a reliable partner for government agencies, offering necessary technological solutions to solve important problems in healthcare provision. Her efforts in this field left behind enhanced access to care for underprivileged groups, increased efficiency, and better healthcare results.

Kang's impact goes beyond her work in healthcare IT to include her promotion of diversity, equity, and inclusion. She broke down obstacles and became a role model for women and minorities in business and technology as a woman of colour working in a mostly white and male sector. Kang's dedication to supporting diversity went beyond mere representation to include giving underprivileged groups chances to flourish. The sector has benefited from her initiatives to empower women of colour in leadership roles, advance mentoring, and expand access to IT and healthcare possibilities. Using her labour, she cleared the path for other women and minorities to pursue professions in fields previously underprivileged, therefore fostering a more varied workforce.

Additionally, defining Kang's legacy is her charitable activities. She has advocated social justice, education, and healthcare access using her success and clout. Countless lives have been improved by her advocacy of education in STEM fields, improvement of healthcare access for underprivileged populations, and support of projects for social justice. Kang's charitable activities are firmly anchored in her conviction that everyone, from all backgrounds or situations, has the chance to flourish. Using mentoring, financial support, or building chances for underprivileged groups, Kang's efforts have enabled many people to follow their aspirations and reach success. Her impact as a philanthropist goes beyond the money she has given to include the significant improvement she has brought about in the lives of people who gain from her work.

Apart from her charitable activities, Kang's support of structural transformation motivates many other leaders to adopt a similar approach.

She has shown that corporate leaders may be successful and socially conscious, as well as that the search for profit should coincide with the quest for constructive social change. Based on Kang's example, businesses can actively support causes that fit their values in addition to their goods and services, therefore transforming the world. Her dedication to social responsibility and ethical leadership has established a new benchmark for corporate executives since it shows that companies can and ought to help create a society that is more fair and equal.

Kang's influence is also shown in her redefining of women's roles in technology and business. Many women, especially women of colour, have been motivated by her tale to explore fields they might have been considered to be closed off to them. Her ascent to prominence in a field that frequently undervalues women has demonstrated how resilient, hardworking, and with the correct assistance, women can overcome obstacles and produce significant influence. Kang's support of gender equality and her leadership in the tech sector have opened doors for a new generation of female leaders transforming sectors and fostering invention.

Regarding her legacy, Michele Kang will be regarded as a trailblazer who not only excelled in her industry but also made chances available for others using her position. Her narrative is one of tenacity in the face of hardship, of leadership with intent, of using her success to inspire others. She has demonstrated that success is about the long-lasting influence one can have on the surroundings as well as about personal accomplishment. Future generations of leaders, activists, and businesspeople dedicated to changing the world will find inspiration in Kang's legacy.

Kang's influence will surely always be a lighthouse as the areas of technology and healthcare keep changing. Her legacy is one of invention, fairness, and compassion toward others. Using her work, Michele Kang has shown that success is most meaningful when it is applied to enhance the lives of others and produce long-lasting, favourable transformation. Whether in activism, philanthropy, or healthcare IT, Kang's contributions have had a significant influence and will help to shape the future for the next generations.

Personal Life

The personal life of Michele Kang is a major component of her narrative; it reflects her values, objectives, and the ideas that have directed her humanitarian activities and career. Renowned for her emphasis on family, community, and advocacy, Kang has deftly negotiated the pressures of corporate leadership while keeping close ties to her background and obligations.

Kang's family has been a pillar of support for her, and her mentality and work ethic have been much shaped by her contacts with them. Growing up in a family that valued education, diligence, and endurance highly, Kang discovered early on the need for morals like discipline, empathy, and resiliency. Her drive to succeed has come from the support and influence of her family; she has also frequently discussed the need to have a solid basis based on mutual respect and confidence. Her time management abilities and dedication to building deep relationships are demonstrated by her capacity to juggle the responsibilities of managing a profitable company while also being a committed mother and wife.

Additionally greatly influencing Kang's perspective and leadership approach is her cultural heritage. She was born in South Korea and early on moved to the United States with her family. Her perspective on the value of diversity and inclusion has changed in response to her experience of adjusting to a foreign nation and the difficulties of doing so. Her own immigrant experiences have stoked her enthusiasm for promoting underprivileged groups—especially women of colour—in business and technology. Kang has frequently discussed how her childhood has affected her leadership style and her dedication to making sure that people from many backgrounds have access to possibilities.

Kang has made it plain that she cherishes her time and deliberately tries to strike a balance between her career and her family life despite her success in the office. She has always given her children priority as a mother and put much effort toward being present for them. Particularly in high-stakes sectors like government contracting and healthcare IT, Kang has candidly addressed the difficulties of being a working mother. She has, however, been able to make sure her family stays a top priority, usually with help from her family and close circle of friends and coworkers. Her ambitious career has been pursued thanks to this balance, which also creates a loving family environment and shows that one may have both personal satisfaction and professional success.

Michele Kang is also quite committed in her own life to philanthropy and community service. Apart from her work obligations, Kang is enthusiastic about returning and has devoted much of her time to many issues connected to diversity, education, and healthcare. She has participated in many projects aiming at giving poor areas access to education and has worked nonstop to support programs aiming at women in leadership roles, especially in sectors like science, technology, engineering, and mathematics (STEM). Her own experiences as a woman of colour in a field dominated by men have motivated her to fight for more support and representation for underprivileged groups, especially in the tech and business sectors.

Kang's personal life likewise shows her commitment to education and personal development. She has made it a point to always broaden her knowledge and skill set over her career as she is a passionate reader and lifetime student. Her dedication to personal growth has shaped her leadership approach and kept her flexible and forward-looking in an often shifting corporate environment. Her company, Cognosante, likewise reflects this never-ending quest for excellence since development and innovation take the front stage.

Understanding that self-care is critical to preserving the vitality and attention required for success, Kang has also given health and well-being priority both personally and professionally. Her schedule is rigorous, but she has made an effort to include wellness in everyday activities. Whether using meditation, physical activity, or time spent with loved ones, Kang understands the need to preserve a good mind and body to support long-term success.

Her personal life also reflects her principles as a leader since she is quite committed to social and environmental issues. Kang has participated in programs meant to increase environmental sustainability and handle public health concerns, including climate change. Her professional job reflects her dedication to these topics since she has constantly advocated for corporate practices with environmental awareness and social responsibility.

Michele Kang's personal life is essentially defined by a strong feeling of family, culture, and social responsibility. Her path as a corporate leader, mother, and immigrant has moulded her into a visionary, kind, and strong person. Notwithstanding her achievements in the field, Kang stays close to her roots and is dedicated to leveraging her personal and business venues to influence society positively. Her capacity to strike a balance between her personal life and her work is evidence of the need to realize harmony between personal gratification and professional achievement.

Conclusion

The life and work of Michele Kang provide a wonderful model of leadership, fortitude, and the force of invention. From her modest immigrant background to her pathfinder in the healthcare IT sector, Kang's story is evidence of the value of diligence, tenacity, and dedication to bring about good change. Her involvement in starting and expanding Cognosante has transformed healthcare technology and established new benchmarks for how government initiatives may use innovative ideas to enhance system efficiency and patient care.

Beyond her work, Kang's narrative is one of strong ties to family, culture, and civic responsibility. Her support of diversity, equity, and inclusion, as well as her charitable endeavours,s, have had a major influence on the lives of innumerable people and neighbourhoods. According to Kang, success is determined by the good impact one makes on others and society as a whole in addition to personal accomplishments.

For the next generations, Kang's legacy will be felt. Combining professional success with a dedication to social change, she has demonstrated how ethical and powerful commercial leadership can be. Through her work, she has motivated many people—especially women and minorities—to follow their interests and remove obstacles in sectors that are sometimes closed off to them. Years to come will be shaped in healthcare, technology, and social justice by her achievements.

Michele Kang's journey is ultimately one of vision, tenacity, and a constant drive to make the world a better place, not only of professional accomplishment. Kang shows, as she keeps motivating people with her example, that one person really can change things with a mix of will, creativity, and equity dedication.

www.ingramcontent.com/pod-product-compliance
Lightning Source LLC
Chambersburg PA
CBHW070417230526
45471CB00006B/2851